THE OFFICIAL TNA IMPACT WRESTLING ANNUAL 2014

WRITTEN BY MATTHEW J. HARDY
PRODUCED BY DEAN DIONYSIOU
DESIGNED BY NICKY REGAN

A Grange Publication

© 2013. Published by Grange Communications Ltd, Edinburgh under licence from
TNA Impact Wrestling. Printed in the EU.

ISBN: 978-1-908925-57-2

£7.99

6-7	JB's Quiz Corner - The Champ is Here!
8-11	Jeff Hardy
12-13	TNA UK Tour 2013
14	British Boot Camp
15	Rockstar Spud
17	One Night Only - X-Travaganza
18	Spot the Difference
19	One Night Only - Joker's Wild
20-21	Bully Ray
22	TNA Crossword
24-26	Knockouts
27	One Night Only - Hardcore Justice 2
29	Wordsearch 1
30-34	Aces & Eights
35	JB's Quiz Corner - TNA Quiz
38-39	Austin Aries
40-41	Bad Influence
42	One Night Only - Tag Team Tournament
43	TNA Maze
44-45	AJ Styles
47	Wordsearch 2
48	Kurt Angle
49	Bobby Roode
50	Kenny King
51	James Storm
52	Guerrero & Hernandez
53	Magnus
54	Sting
55	Hulk Hogan
58-59	Abyss to Joseph Park
60-61	Answers
62-63	Where's Bobby Roode?

CONTENTS

1

2

JB'S QUIZ CORNER (GUESS WHO?)

THE CHAMP IS

5

6

3

4

ERE!

JEREMY BORASH: Since its creation in 2007, thirteen different TNA superstars have held the coveted TNA World Heavyweight Championship. Can you work out which former or former TNA World Champions are disguised in these 8 images? Write your answers in the spaces provided and then check your answers at the back of this book (P60-61).

7

8

PROFILE 'THE CHARISMATIC ENIGMA'

JEFF HARDY

(@JEFFHARDYBRAND)

HEIGHT: 6'2"

WEIGHT: 215LBS

FROM: Cameron, North Carolina

FINISHING MOVE: The Swanton

To his millions of followers around the world, who Jeff affectionately refers to as his 'Creatures of the Night', he is the epitome of a TNA superstar. Sharing in the many highs and occasional lows throughout Jeff's career, their devotion to him and his devotion to his 'Creatures' is an unbreakable bond.

And over the last year in TNA Wrestling, Jeff Hardy has shown he deserves every bit of their adulation by capturing the TNA World Heavyweight title for the third time.

On October 14th, 2012, at TNA's biggest show of the year, Bound For Glory, Jeff realised his dream of recapturing the world title in a gripping one-on-one contest against then champion Austin Aries.

It marked the culmination of a personal 'Road to Redemption' for Jeff, having come back from a myriad of personal and professional setbacks which had tested the resolve of 'The Charismatic Enigma'.

Earning this World title match alone, proved Jeff Hardy was back to his best as was shown by winning the 'Bound For Glory' Series held over the previous four months. Finishing in fourth place in the league-style format entered Hardy into a semi-final match with Samoa Joe, another man on his own mini revival. In the final Jeff would battle his long-term adversary Bully Ray. A Swanton Bomb later and Jeff Hardy had booked his place versus Austin Aries for the World Heavyweight Championship. The rest is history.

"JEFF HARDY HAS SHOWN HE DESERVES EVERY BIT OF THEIR ADULATION BY CAPTURING THE TNA WORLD HEAVYWEIGHT TITLE FOR THE THIRD TIME."

As champion, you always have a target on your back and for Jeff, it was no different. But dazzling rematches with Aries in the following months and other successful defences against the likes of Christopher Daniels, Kurt Angle and Bobby Roode, cemented Hardy in his position at the head of the TNA locker room.

At Lockdown in the spring, Bully Ray would once again prove the challenger and headlined against Jeff inside of a steel cage. Though there had always been the threat that underground faction Aces & Eights would get involved in their match, Jeff felt confident that he and Bully, whilst rivals in the match, would unite to fend off the group should the need arise.

They both had issues with the leather-clad group, so when Aces & Eights appeared during the main event at Lockdown, the wrestling world was stunned when Aces & Eights member Devon handed his half-brother Bully Ray a weapon with which Ray knocked out Hardy. The resulting pin might have earned Bully Ray the World title but it also stoked the fires inside Jeff Hardy.

In the ring, Jeff Hardy's drive and determination manifests itself through a daredevil attitude and a 'never-say-die' spirit that few in professional wrestling can match. Now more hungry than ever to climb the ladder and reclaim the World Heavyweight Championship, Jeff has the odds stacked against him but rest assured, he has overcome massive obstacles in the past. Time will tell whether Aces & Eights proves one obstacle too many.

TNA

"AS CHAMPION, YOU ALWAYS HAVE A TARGET ON YOUR BACK AND FOR JEFF, IT WAS NO DIFFERENT."

Back to the UK for the fifth time, the 2013 instalment of the Maximum Impact Tour saw TNA Impact Wrestling head to Dublin, Glasgow, Nottingham, Manchester and London on consecutive nights in January. Welcomed by thousands of wild, enthusiastic and informed fans, TNA put on shows like no other.

The stars were out in the UK as world class wrestling from the brightest young performers in the industry and guest appearances from legends like Sting and Hulk Hogan, meant TNA's UK fans got more than their money's worth.

To top it all off, the fans in attendance at Wembley Arena in London were once again treated to two episodes of TNA's flagship show, Impact Wrestling, taped before their very eyes. But whether the events are to be televised around the world, or are just for those lucky enough to be in the arena, TNA guarantees all fans a fantastic evening of entertainment and spectacle. For TNA, the UK is a second home and the tour represents a thank you from TNA to its UK fans for their continued support.

Year on year, the Impact of TNA wrestling in the UK is getting bigger and bigger. Earlier tours in smaller venues have paved the way for sell-out arena tours in the biggest cities in the UK and Ireland. The Maximum Impact Tour V added another chapter to the love affair which will continue into 2014 with Maximum Impact Tour VI.

The 2014 Maximum Impact Tour VI is already on sale and no doubt fans will be back supporting their favourite TNA wrestlers. And as a special thanks to fans in Glasgow, this year Impact Wrestling will be broadcast live to the nation on Challenge TV from the brand new Hydro Arena. It'll be a historical moment for TNA, Glasgow and Challenge TV. Make sure to book your place on the TNA Maximum Impact Tour 2014 early to avoid disappointment.

Check out the 2014 tour advert on page 16 to find out how you can be a part of TNA wrestling.

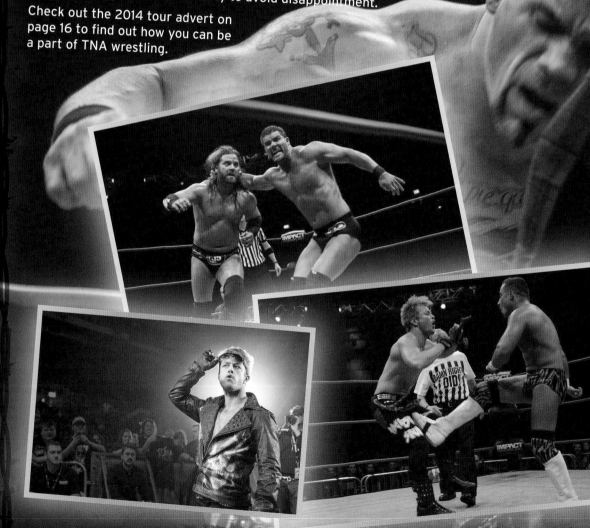

"MAKE SURE TO BOOK YOUR PLACE ON THE TNA MAXIMUM IMPACT TOUR 2014 EARLY TO AVOID DISAPPOINTMENT."

TNA
UK
TOUR 2013

Since British legend Norman Smiley appeared on the very first episode of TNA in 2002, TNA has had a history of signing the very best UK wrestling talent to their already gifted roster. And who can blame them, with the wealth of talent available waiting to be unearthed on these shores?

From the pioneer for British talent in TNA, Douglas Williams, to the current crop of UK stars including Magnus and 'Big Rob' Terry; TNA has always been a natural home for our home-grown superstars. So it came as no surprise when TNA announced its search for the next superstar of British wrestling to join the TNA ranks.

In partnership with Challenge TV, TNA British Boot Camp debuted on January 1st 2013. The UK exclusive reality-style show gave four up-and-coming British wrestlers the opportunity to win themselves a life changing contract with TNA Impact Wrestling. The Blossom Twins (Hannah & Holly), Marty Scurll and Rockstar Spud, competed against one another over 6 shows, aiming to impress TNA bosses and top officials both inside the ring and outside the ring. Cameras followed the four young talents on this journey from their humble beginnings on the British wrestling scene, as they were put through their paces at the TNA developmental system in Ohio, where they received

mentorship and advice from British and American greats like Mark 'Rollerball' Rocco, Al Snow, Taz and Hulk Hogan. With so much at stake, tensions predictably ran high, especially between Marty and Spud. In their one-on-one encounter on the final episode of British Bootcamp, it was Marty Scurll who won the battle with a 'Death Valley Driver', however, it would be Rockstar Spud who ultimately won the war. The final decision ultimately came down to TNA President Dixie Carter and Hulk Hogan who were suitably impressed by all four of the individuals on show, but in the end, Rockstar Spud emerged victorious and earned a TNA wrestling contract.

"IN PARTNERSHIP WITH CHALLENGE TV, TNA BRITISH BOOT CAMP DEBUTED ON JANUARY 1ST 2013."

BRITISH BOOT CAMP

TNA WRESTLING

BRITISH BOOT CAMP

The 29 year old Brummie has been making waves on the British wrestling scene for a decade. He may be one of, if not 'the' smallest wrestler on the circuit, but what Spud lacks in size, he makes up for in passion, ability and charisma. Spud always had 'it'.

He was just waiting for a chance to show the world, and that chance came when TNA came and offered him a part on 'British Boot Camp'.

Rockstar Spud, with his sunglasses, leopard print accessories, chains and leather, looks **the** part. But Rockstar is not just a name; it's a way of life. Spud can be loud, obnoxious and in your face, but as British Boot Camp showed, deep down he is just a kid with a dream. A dream which he fulfilled by winning a TNA contract and then going on to compete on the Maximum Impact Tour where he debuted for TNA at Wembley Arena by defeating Robbie E.

In the months that followed Rockstar Spud has been honing his skills with TNA, waiting for his moment to come to be unleashed in TNA.

It is a moment that can't come soon enough for many UK fans eager to see another of their countrymen rock TNA Impact Wrestling.

TNA

"SPUD CAN BE LOUD, OBNOXIOUS AND IN YOUR FACE."

PROFILE
ROCKSTAR SPUD (@ROCKSTARSPUD)

HEIGHT: 5'4"

WEIGHT: 130LBS

FROM: BIRMINGHAM, ENGLAND

FINISHING MOVE: ROCKSTAR STUNNER

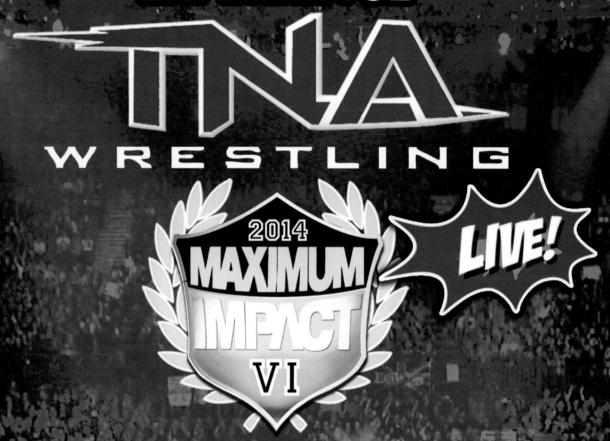

EXPERIENCE TNA WRESTLING

2014 MAXIMUM IMPACT VI

LIVE!

WEDNESDAY 29 JANUARY	DUBLIN NATIONAL STADIUM
THURSDAY 30 JANUARY	GLASGOW HYDRO
FRIDAY 31 JANUARY	MANCHESTER ARENA
SATURDAY 01 FEBRUARY	LONDON WEMBLEY ARENA
SUNDAY 02 FEBRUARY	BIRMINGHAM NIA

TNA
ONE NIGHT ONLY
05.04.13 X-TRAVAGANZA

In 2013, TNA introduced a new pay-per-view concept, which it would call TNA: One Night Only. The idea was to offer TNA fans something new and something different that they could not see anywhere else on TNA programming.

One Night Only would be a series of one-off, themed events highlighting a particular area of the TNA product. The first of these events, which air in the UK on Challenge TV, was entitled X-Travaganza.

Airing in April 2013, X-Travaganza featured the stars of TNA's very popular and ground breaking X Division. The X Division, created at the birth of TNA, was a division in which superstars could show the world what they could do regardless of size. The XDivision was 'not about weight limits, it was about no limits', and gave us some of the greatest feuds and matches in TNA Wrestling history. Who can forget Austin Aries 301 day title reign, or the three-way feud between AJ Styles, Samoa Joe and Christopher Daniels in 2005, or the feud which put TNA on the map between AJ Styles and Jerry Lynn in the early days of the company? At X-Travaganza, TNA brought together stars of past and present for one unforgettable night.

MATCHES

- Christian York def. Alex Silva, Jimmy Rave, Lince Dorado, Matt Bentley, Puma & Sam Shaw in an Xscape match

- Douglas Williams & Kid Kash def. Rashad Cameron & Anthony Nease

- Chavo Guerrero def. Robbie E

- Kenny King def. Zema Ion, Rubix & Mason Andrews in an Ultimate X match

- Bad Influence (Christopher Daniels & Kazarian) def. Petey Williams & Sonjay Dutt

- Rob Van Dam def. Jerry Lynn in a No DQ match

- Main Event - Austin Aries def. Samoa Joe

SPOT THE DIFFERENCE

Can you spot the 10 differences in these pics? Answers on page 60-61

TNA

ONE NIGHT ONLY

03.05.13 JOKER'S WILD

The second One Night Only event was called Joker's Wild. The premise was based around a popular WCW (World Championship Wrestling) concept from the early 1990s called 'Lethal Lottery'. As such, at Joker's Wild, 24 men competed to win $100,000, in a tournament like no other. In phase one of the night, individual wrestlers were teamed up in random selections to make 'One Night Only' tag teams.

The potential for controversy was huge. We could see friend versus friend, foe versus foe, or maybe even regular tag team partners split on opposing teams. Whatever the case, partners would have to work together if they wanted to advance. The winners of these two-on-two tag team contests would then progress to the main event... a 12-man Battle Royal, where they had a chance to win $100,000.

MATCHES

- James Storm & Christian York def. Crimson & Gunner

- Mr. Anderson & Jessie Godderz def. Douglas Williams & Kid Kash

- Samoa Joe & Christopher Daniels def. Chavo Guerrero & Rob Van Dam

- Bobby Roode & Joseph Park def. Robbie E. & Zema Ion

- Devon & D.O.C. def. Hernandez & Alex Silva

- Matt Morgan & Rob Terry def. Al Snow & Joey Ryan

- Main Event Battle Royal – James Storm outlasted Samoa Joe, Christopher Daniels, Mr. Anderson, D.O.C., Devon, Jessie Godderz, Christian York, Bobby Roode, Joseph Park, Matt Morgan & Rob Terry

When Bully Ray and Jeff Hardy stood back to back inside the steel cage at Lockdown 2013, few could see what would happen next. Instead of helping to fight off the incoming Aces & Eights, Bully Ray was the benefactor of a ball-pin hammer, passed to him by his half-brother and Sgt. At Arms Devon, which he cracked over the head of the defending champion, before covering Hardy for the win. The final piece of the jigsaw was in place, and the President of Aces & Eights was revealed. Most importantly, TNA had a new World Heavyweight Champion, and not one to be proud of.

PROFILE PRESIDENT, ACES & EIGHTS

BULLY RAY

(@REALBULLY5150)

HEIGHT: 6'4"

WEIGHT: 326lbs

FROM: Hell's Kitchen, New York

FINISHING MOVE: The Bully Bomb

You can read the full story of how Aces & Eights evolved elsewhere in this annual, but in trying to shift the gaze of the TNA audience to deceive them of his true role, Bully Ray carved his own dastardly route to the title.

Always entangled in the Aces & Eights feud, the finger would often be pointed at Bully Ray as the man behind the group. Somehow Bully always managed to deflect attention towards some other poor wrestler. So keen was Bully Ray to convince us and Hulk Hogan that he was on the side of TNA that he often fought with members of the group. But when it was revealed that Bully Ray had begun a secret affair with Hogan's daughter Brooke, it seemed he had overstepped the mark. Hogan suspended the pair the next week. But it appeared that their love ran much deeper and the more Hulk protested, the more she fell for Bully Ray. On an episode of Impact Wrestling, Bully proposed to Brooke Hogan and she accepted.

Probably realising he had no right to dictate who his daughter could date, Hogan slowly began to trust Ray after seeing him rush to his and his daughter's aid on more than one occasion. Given Hulk's blessing, the wedding on Impact Wrestling was supposed to be a joyous day but Aces & Eights again interrupted. Hogan reinstated Bully to team with Sting and challenge the group. After the match that they had won, Hogan handed Ray the number one contender's spot to face Jeff Hardy for the TNA heavyweight title at Lockdown. It may have been a touch of nepotism on Hulk's part towards his new son-in-law, and it proved to be a big mistake. As Bully Ray held aloft the TNA title after the match at Lockdown, he screamed 'Hulk, I USED you. I am the President of the Aces & Eights, and I am the TNA World Heavyweight Champion.'

> "THE MORE HULK PROTESTED, THE MORE SHE FELL FOR BULLY RAY. "

TNA CROSSWORD

Answers on page 60

ACROSS

1 TNA's ring announcer. (6,6)

4 When someone interferes in a match, the result is a _____. (16)

6 Christopher Daniels & Kazarian are a _____. (3,9)

8 Event where TNA celebrates its birthday. (13)

11 The home of TNA on British TV. (9)

12 The place to go in Europe for all your TNA merchandising needs. (9)

15 The leader of the selfish generation. (5,5)

16 The UK city from where Impact will be shown live in 2014. (7)

17 The leader of the group in Clue 2. (5,3)

18 The UK-born Gladiator. (6)

DOWN

2 The group who invaded TNA in 2012/13. (4,3,6)

3 Full Metal _____, a tables, chairs and ladders match in TNA. (6)

5 The longest reigning TNA Knockouts champion in history. (4,3)

7 Park & _____, the law firm owned by Joseph Park. (10)

9 Venue which TNA called home during its early years. (6)

10 The winner of British Boot Camp. (8,4)

13 Open _____ Night, when anyone in TNA can challenge anyone. (5)

14 _____ Wild, TNA's second One Night Only event. (6)

The dictionary describes a knockout as either an act of leaving somebody unconscious or a strikingly attractive person. In TNA, the two meanings are combined into packages we call the TNA Knockouts. As a prized part of Impact Wrestling, the women's Knockouts Division is not just about beauties with sex appeal, it's about assertive, strong vixens who are as tough, mean and talented in the ring as their male counterparts.

TNA SPOTLIGHT ON THE TNA KNOCKOUTS

VELVET SKY

(@VELVELHOLLER)

Velvet Sky has come a long way since her time as part of the most infamous female stables in professional wrestling, "The Beautiful People" with Angelina Love. Displaying impressive submission skills, Sky embarked on her pursuit of the TNA Knockouts title which she won on the biggest night of her life at Bound For Glory 2011. Velvet Sky outlasted Mickie James, Madison Rayne and champion Winter in a four-way tussle that night to capture her first singles Championship.

Whilst a first title win for any competitor is an amazing moment, winning that second championship arguably solidifies your position as the real deal. There couldn't have been a greater time for Velvet Sky to capture her second TNA Knockouts title than in London's Wembley Arena. In front of a jam packed house, Sky defeated Tara, Miss Tessmacher and Gail Kim in a Fatal Four-Way match, repeating her achievements of two years prior.

Though Velvet Sky lost the title to Mickie James, Velvet Sky remains ever popular with the TNA faithful and no doubt hopes that with their help, this beautiful person can reach for the Sky once more.

TARYN TERRELL

(@THETARYNTERRELL)

Outside of the ring, Taryn Terrell has a long list of impressive accomplishments as a former actress (in HBO's 'Treme' and movies such as 'The Campaign') and even as a stuntwoman. The latter role must have given Terrell a thirst for action as she now grapples with the gals of TNA. It was perhaps inevitable that her career as a Knockouts' referee would not last as she is far more at home at the centre of trouble than as the mediator. Perhaps she has barked up the wrong tree in upsetting future Knockouts' Hall of Famer Gail Kim, but as we have already seen from Terrell's early forays in the ring, she can more than hold her own. If her development continues at the same pace as it's begun, we predict the stunning blonde will be wearing Knockouts gold around her waist in the not too distant future.

GAIL KIM

(@GAILKIMITSME)

Gail Kim is still the alpha female in TNA Wrestling. Though she may not always be Knockouts champion, she is 100% b*tch, 24/7 if you dare to cross her. And then... the gloves are off, as Taryn Terrell found out earlier this year.

Terrell as Knockout's referee cost Kim a Knockouts' title match when she failed to see Kim's foot under the bottom rope. Taking this personally, Kim verbally attacked Terrell but it proved a bad move as Taryn Terrell gained retribution by again costing Kim the Knockouts title in a later match. There was no confusion this time however, as Terrell physically assaulted the Canadian-Korean beauty. The back and forth between the two led to Terrell being fired as referee by Brooke Hogan but immediately hired as a wrestler. Kim and Terrell were on a collision course. Though it was Terrell who got the upper hand in their first few encounters, Gail Kim is a wily veteran of the squared circle and will no doubt be back to teach the impulsive youngster some harsh lessons.

One thing we know about Kim is that she has been around the business long enough to know how to play every situation. In the ring, her technical ability is matched by her intelligence and whilst she may sometimes lose the battle, Gail Kim has shown over time that she will always win the war. Taryn Terrell better watch out.

MISS TESSMACHER
(@BROOKETESS)

Miss Tessmacher certainly lives up to the name 'Knockout'. Having won over 20 beauty pageant titles in her life, some doubted whether she had the in-ring ability to go with her stunning looks. Since debuting as Eric Bischoff's sexy assistant, Miss Tessmacher has honed her skills in the ring to become a match for any woman on the TNA roster. This was never more evident than when, as a member of the team 'TnT' with Tara, Brooke Tessmacher won her first TNA championship to become one half of the Knockouts Tag Team Champions. As a singles star, she proved her advancement still further by pinning the legendary Knockouts champion Gail Kim to lift the TNA Knockouts championship. Though she would eventually lose the strap, the heart and determination Brooke showed between the ropes earned her another championship by defeating Madison Rayne. Now a former 2-time TNA Knockouts champion, Miss Tessmacher is never far from the title picture and with her growing fan base willing her on, title number three may be just around the corner.

MICKIE JAMES
(@MICKIEJAMES)

With a decade of experience under her belt, the North American Knockout legend Mickie James is one of the cornerstones of the TNA Knockouts division and the barometer which all other Knockouts compare themselves against. Though Mickie James took a 3 month hiatus from TNA, she came back with the goal of reaching the top once more. Frustrated in the months that followed by several failed attempts to win the Knockouts title, fans began to notice an attitude shift in their beloved star. This was fully realised when James finally won her third Knockouts title in a hard fought contest with Velvet Sky. The relief was evident, but in her successful rematch against Sky, the change in mindset reared its ugly head as she left her opponent to get beat down in a post match attack by Gail Kim. Could this mean an alliance between the two most dominant divas in TNA? One thing we know is that Mickie James will do everything in her power to hold onto the gold.

BROOKE HOGAN
(@MIZZHOGAN)

No one could blame Brooke Hogan for questioning why she followed her father into the wrestling industry. It's a business ingrained in the family, but it has led to much heartache for Brooke this year.

All seemed to be going so well when she was Head of the Knockouts Division and had fallen for the popular and courageous Bully Ray. Though she knew her father would not approve, her heart longed for Ray and when he proposed marriage, she was the happiest she had ever been. Even when the wedding was interrupted by renegade group 'Aces & Eights', Brooke still could not have foreseen that the man she married was playing her, her father and the whole wrestling world just to get the TNA World title. Though betrayed by Bully Ray, Brooke has not shied away for the spotlight. When she finally gets her hands on her estranged husband, this Hogan is going to run wild all over Bully Ray.

TNA
ONE NIGHT ONLY
05.07.13 HARDCORE JUSTICE 2

The original Hardcore Justice occurred in 2010, billed as one last stand of the old hardcore fraternity. Taking over the usual Hard Justice PPV slot, the event was renamed and as the name suggests, a hardcore element was inserted to all of the matches. In 2013, the themed PPV resurfaced for another all action, weapons-filled extravaganza. With several faces from TNA's past coming back, and a couple of well-known stars of yesteryear on this extreme showcase, this was a One Night Only event for a number of reasons.

MATCHES

- ODB def. Jackie Moore in a Hardcore Knockouts match

- LAX (Homicide & Hernandez) def. The Disciples of the New Church (Slash & Sinn)

- Bad Influence def. Generation Me in a Tag Team Ladder match

- Shark Boy outlasted Devon Storm, Little Guido, Crimson, Sam Shaw, Funaki, Johnny Swinger, Gunner and 2 Cold Scorpio in a Hardcore Gauntlet Battle Royal

- James Storm, Magnus & Bob Holly def. Aces & Eights (D.O.C, Knux & Wes Brisco) in a 6-Man Elimination match

- Joseph Park def. Judas Mesias in a Monsters Ball match

- Main Event - Jeff Hardy & Brother Runt def. Team 3D (Bully Ray & Devon) in a Tag Team Tables match

FIGHT!
WORDSEARCH

Find the words in the grid. Words can go horizontally, vertically and diagonally in all eight directions. Answers on page 61.

ADouble
Blueprint
BullyRay
CharismaticEnigma
Cowboy
FallenAngel
Icon
Immortal
Monster
Phenomenal
Professor
RockStar
SamoanSubmissionMachine
SuperMex

```
Z N R J Y Y Q N F C R Z N E K L B P C N T D F
X K H W Y T N Z V K M H G N T L M N D H C C K
H I M M O R T A L H G L L I Y T N Y V Z B R P
K K W L Q X Q A R W K Z P H D R A T S K C O R
N C H M D T R M W R B R F C T M K L R C M E W
D K W B R X P G X V W M N A H N K R L K T T P
N B L M M K R I P Y A F J M Y N I J F S H C N
K N H J M N O N L P D T W N M D H R N N B T Q
T H K R Q K F E H G O K T O Q F Q O P Y N X Z
H N D D J C E C L K U X R I M X M X K E N M W
K R V F X B S I J P B X Q S Z F N M N M U M Z
T P B M K V S T X B L Y G S N Z Q Q C Y P L K
M N D U K G O A P F E N Y I L L B L T C K C B
P R C P L T R M H M L N N M F C O W B O Y R F
L H N M Q L Z S X B O T H B C T W B C Y C P L
K Z E F M D Y I L C W Y L U M Q N G S M C G N
R D T N V K R R I M F B L S V V M U N L M G T
R J J X O P D A A L V W K N V L P T Q L T F K
K T L P M M M W H Y Y K K N A T E M Y Y M T M T
T L B D W J E C R Q L J J O R W T J M X P T X
L T F A L L E N A N G E L M T D C Q R P N T R
Q M W W W N T L A R K C E A T W J F K K R R P
M B H X D M F C R L R X T S X M N W T K T L B
```

29

What's in a name? Wrestling factions have long been known for having unusual names; Immortal, Fortune, Team Canada (OK not the last one). But Aces & Eights is not just a cool sounding stable nickname. You can guess that it's got something to do with playing cards, but what does it mean? Well, behind this name is a fascinating true story.

The year is 1876. It was a warm summer evening in the gold-mining town of Deadwood, in the Black Hills of South Dakota, a town celebrated by the HBO/Sky1 series of the same name. 'Wild' Bill Hickok, a famed lawman of the time, walks into the Nuttal & Mann's Saloon to waste the evening away on his favourite pastime, poker. Hickok's work had often led to him amassing many enemies and so he would usually sit with his back to the wall to get a view of the room and any persons who might wish to cause him harm. On this night, he was joining the poker game late and only one chair remained, with its back to the room. After requests to change seats fell on deaf ears, 'Wild Bill' took the remaining seat and settled in to the game of poker.

Jack McCall, who had played poker with Hickok the previous evening and lost a significant amount of money, wandered unnoticed into the bar as Bill's attention was focused on the game. In retaliation for Hickok's condescending remarks that morning at breakfast about the money he lost the previous evening, McCall drew his pistol and without

hesitation, fired a single round at 'Wild' Bill Hickok. The bullet killed Hickok instantly.

What does this have to do with Aces & Eights? When 'Wild Bill' Hickok was shot and killed by Jack McCall, he was holding a poker hand containing two Aces and two Eights, all of which were black (clubs and spades). This hand was immortalised at the time of his death and 'Aces & Eights' became known as the 'Dead Man's Hand'.

In TNA, the group known as 'Aces & Eights' pay homage to this moment in American History every night they perform.

The back and forth match between TNA World Heavyweight Champion Jeff Hardy and Bully Ray could have gone either way. The two fan favourites had been going full pelt in the Lockdown cage for over 15 minutes and had already withheld the first onslaught by 'Aces & Eights' members Wes Brisco and Garett Bischoff. It seemed that one way or another Hardy and Ray would decide this title match fair and square and Ace & Eights were not going to spoil the party. But it wasn't long before the whole of the renegade group had the ring and the two competitors surrounded. As they attempted to enter the ring, Sgt-at-Arms Devon stood on the top turnbuckle producing a hammer to seemingly attack Bully Ray and Jeff Hardy. But in the ultimate swerve on the watching audience and on Jeff Hardy himself, Devon threw the hammer to Ray to use to knock out the defending champion.

> "A NEW TNA WORLD HEAVYWEIGHT CHAMPION WAS CROWNED."

ACES & EIGHTS

A HISTORY LESSON

Bully Ray covered Jeff Hardy and a new TNA World Heavyweight Champion was crowned.

We first met the group who we would later call 'Aces & Eights' on June 14th 2012 when three masked assailants would viciously assault 'The Icon' Sting during an in-ring speech reacting to his pending Hall of Fame induction. Over the following weeks and months, the group grew in number and would continue to interfere in matches on Impact Wrestling and PPVs. Though the identities of the attackers were not known at this point, they wore masks; we learned of their name by a delivery of a photo of four playing cards in an envelope to Hulk Hogan. 'Aces & Eights' was born.

No TNA superstar was immune from becoming a victim of the TNA invaders. Names on the Aces & Eights hit list included Jeff Hardy, Samoa Joe, Austin Aries, Kurt Angle, Sting, Hulk Hogan and even Bully Ray himself. All found themselves on the wrong end of numerous beatings. As we would find out at Lockdown 2013, the attacks on Bully Ray were just a cover, to hide the true intentions of the group and the true mastermind and president of Aces & Eights. The 'Plan A' was for Bully Ray to win the Bound For Glory series. Coincidentally all attacks undeniably profited Bully although it was not obvious at the time. The insinuation that James Storm was Aces' leader also simmered the heat on Bully Ray. However, the heart of Jeff Hardy proved a stumbling block in the plan that Ray could not overcome.

> **" ALL FOUND THEMSELVES ON THE WRONG END OF NUMEROUS BEATINGS."**

It was Hardy who would beat Bully Ray to win the BFG series and earn the TNA World title shot.

Flying under the radar of security in the Impact Zone, Aces & Eights members pounced whenever the moment took them, but as resistance started to mount, they orchestrated a match for Bound For Glory whereby if Aces & Eights won, they would be granted unrestricted access to the arena. If they lost, they would disband and leave TNA. In hindsight, up against Sting & Bully Ray, this was probably never going to happen. In a competitive match up, which with his participation, again had the aim of deflecting heat from Bully Ray, Aces & Eights emerged victorious following outside interference from another masked member of the group. This man was later revealed as Devon, the half brother of Bully Ray and the man that many believed had left TNA for good earlier in the year whilst still recognised as TNA TV Champion.

Devon, the Sergeant-at-Arms of Aces & Eights, believed he had been mistreated and disrespected by TNA management and Hulk Hogan in particular. He had a point. The veteran's contract had been left to expire without a new one being offered. Two weeks later, the Director of Chaos was unmasked. Known simply as D.O.C., this familiar face was further evidence that Aces & Eights meant business. He, and the later reveal of Knux, provided Aces with muscle in the group and demonstrated that this was a group of talented athletes not solely at odds with TNA, but the whole wrestling industry.

As more of the TNA talent roster fell victim to the group, one man decided that if he couldn't beat them, then he would join them. Mr. Anderson, as a former TNA World Champion was perhaps the biggest defection to the faction.

After Taz shocked the world and joined Aces during the Bully Ray/Brooke Hogan wedding, Garett Bischoff and Wes Brisco identified themselves as the latest members of the 'Dead Man's Hand' group. Bischoff was another with a grievance with Hulk Hogan, feeling he was unfairly shunned on TV when he had been nothing but supportive of Hogan against his father Eric Bischoff in 2012. Attacking Kurt Angle, Bischoff paved the way for a two-on-one assault, as Wes Brisco, Kurt's protégé suddenly joined the frenzy.

It had been Kurt Angle who had got Brisco a shot on the Gut Check Challenge in late 2012 but as it would transpire, it was a 7th member of A&E that cast the deciding vote to earn Brisco a TNA contract. D'Lo Brown was on the judging panel that night, filling in for Al Snow who had mysteriously gone AWOL.

"ONE MAN DECIDED THAT IF HE COULDN'T BEAT THEM, THEN HE WOULD JOIN THEM."

So the Gut Check panel, unbeknownst to the audience was made up of two Aces & Eights members (Taz & D'Lo), voting for a third member, Wes Brisco, who had just beaten a fourth member, Garett Bischoff in his Gut Check Challenge match.

WES BRISCO
(@WESBRISCO)

HEIGHT: 5'10"
WEIGHT: 225LBS
FROM: TAMPA, FLORIDA
FINISHING MOVE: THE BRISCO ROLL

GARETT BISCHOFF
(@GARETTBISCHOFF)

HEIGHT: 6'2"
WEIGHT: 225LBS
FROM: CLEAR WATER BEACH, FLORIDA
FINISHING MOVE: SNAPMARE DRIVER

MR. ANDERSON
(@MRKENANDERSON)

HEIGHT: 6'2"
WEIGHT: 243LBS
FROM: GREEN BAY, WISCONSIN
FINISHING MOVE: THE GREEN BAY PLUNGE

DEVON
(@TESTIFYDEVON)

HEIGHT: 6'2"
WEIGHT: 280LBS
FROM: NEW YORK, NEW YORK
FINISHING MOVE: SPINEBUSTER

The intricate plan was almost fully revealed. So long had this been planned that only once it was over could we stand back and see how fiendish but equally brilliant, the Aces & Eights story was. Every member and every reveal served a purpose. Every member took a beating from the TNA locker room, or from their own Aces & Eights teammates, for the sole purpose of protecting the leader's identity and at Lockdown, the master plan was complete. Bully Ray was the TNA World Heavyweight Champion and the leader behind the most diabolical group in TNA history.

"EVERY MEMBER TOOK A BEATING FROM THE TNA LOCKER ROOM, OR FROM THEIR OWN ACES & EIGHTS TEAMMATES"

IMPACT WRESTLING

1 Which TNA Superstar had the longest single TNA World Heavyweight Championship reign in 2012, at 256 days?

2 Who was the first unmasked member of Aces & Eights?

3 Name the first and second inductees into the TNA Hall of Fame.

4 What is the name of the One Night Only event featuring only women?

5 Where does Magnus call home?

6 Where do TNA perform when in London?

7 What day of the week does TNA Impact Wrestling first air in the UK and on what channel is it on?

8 Who were the two female competitors featured in the British Boot Camp series?

9 Taz and which other former extreme wrestler were at the wedding ceremony of Bully Ray and Brooke Hogan?

10 What is the name of Chris Sabin's former tag team with Alex Shelley?

11 Christopher Daniels and who, make up the team of Bad Influence?

12 Who is the voice of TNA?

13 Name the four MAIN PPV events.

14 Which wrestler won the Gut Check Final at the June PPV?

15 Name the referee-turned-wrestler who feuded with Gail Kim in 2013?

Check out the answers on page 61 to see just how tough you are on TNA! (One point for each correct answer).

JB'S QUIZ CORNER
TNA QUIZ

FIGHT!

SCORE RATING

20 Correct = You are an honourary inductee of the TNA Hall of Fame.

15-19 = Hulk Hogan says you can be co-general manager of Impact wrestling.

10-14 = The decision is going to the Gut Check Panel... you just made it.

5-9 = Ouch, must do better. Kurt Angle is waiting to snap on the ankle lock.

0-4 = You need to go back and see the Professor, Mike Tenay.

36

He is 'The Greatest Man Who Ever Lived.' At least that's what he'll tell you. Although it's the most outrageous statement someone could bestow upon themselves, it's hard to argue that Austin Aries isn't at least one of the greatest performers in TNA today.

Having the single longest reign as X Division champion (298 days) was not enough to quell the hunger burning deep inside of 'A -Double'. With the greatest respect to the X Division, from day one, Austin Aries had always set his sights on the highest prize... the TNA World Heavyweight Championship.

PROFILE 'THE GREATEST MAN WHO EVER LIVED'
AUSTIN ARIES

(@AUSTINARIES)

HEIGHT: 5'9"

WEIGHT: 210lbs

FROM: Milwaukee, Wisconsin

FINISHING MOVE: Brainbuster/Last Chancery

So confident in his own ability was Austin Aries, that when given the opportunity to surrender his X Division strap for a shot at the World title, he did so without a second thought. Untested in the top echelons, it was a big gamble in the eyes of many, but for Aries it paid off. In what many at the time considered an upset, Austin Aries beat Bobby Roode at Destination X 2012 to capture the TNA World title.

As champion and challenger, Aries and Roode continued their rivalry through the summer of 2012 until Aries' successful reign was ended when he lost the title to Jeff Hardy at Bound For Glory. Returning to his arrogant and self-aggrandising ways, Austin Aries tried every mind game and devilish trick in the book to knock Hardy off his game but in each subsequent rematch, Aries just came up short.

But through his failed attempts against Hardy, his rivalry with Bobby Roode persisted as both men argued amongst themselves as to who should really be number one contender. The Impact Zone was barely big enough for the two egos on display.

However, it seemed to all but the two involved that Austin Aries and Bobby Roode had more in common than they themselves would admit and when Hulk Hogan decided to force Aries and Roode to team together on the Maximum Impact Tour of the UK against tag team champions, Chavo Guerrero and Hernandez, few were surprised when this dysfunctional alliance won gold.

There was never any doubting the talent of the two former world champions and in realising their collective strength as a team, Aries and Roode have been able to co-exist long enough during matches to become a highly effective tag team who should be a force in the division for as long as they can get along.

Winning the tag team titles has meant Austin Aries has become only the fifth man in TNA history to be a Triple Crown winner. He still might not be 'the greatest man in the world', but he is building the resumé of future TNA Hall of Famer.

"THE IMPACT ZONE WAS BARELY BIG ENOUGH FOR THE TWO EGOS ON DISPLAY."

PROFILE
BAD INFLUENCE

It could be argued that parents should stop their children from watching this top tag duo. They are of course a 'Bad Influence'. But when all is said and done, love them or hate them, the team of Christopher Daniels and Kazarian are just too darn entertaining. It's led many fans to list Bad Influence as their guilty pleasure.

CHRISTOPHER DANIELS
(@FACDANIELS)

HEIGHT: 6'0"

WEIGHT: 224lbs

FROM: The City of Angels, California

FINISHING MOVE: BME (Best Moonsault Ever) Chancery

KAZARIAN
(@FRANKIEKAZARIAN)

HEIGHT: 6'1"

WEIGHT: 215lbs

FROM: Anaheim, California

FINISHING MOVE: The Flux Capacitor

"THEY ARE ALSO NOT AFRAID TO THROW IN A CHEAP SHOT WHEN THE REF'S BACK IS TURNED."

Both men are veterans of the TNA ring and veterans of wrestling in general with over 35 years' experience in the ring between them. Daniels and Kazarian had previously held multiple X Division titles (Daniels 3 times, Kazarian 5 times) and are considered two of the pioneers of the division in its heyday. They have been singles opponents and rival members of opposing tag teams but in 2012, a mutual appreciation of each other's mischievous deeds drew the two together to form the team later known as Bad Influence.

Christopher Daniels is renowned as one of the finest in-ring performers of his generation and perhaps one of the best technically sound wrestlers to never hold a world title. Able to chain wrestle the hell out of opponents much bigger than himself, he is also adept going to the top rope. See his 'Best Moonsault Ever' as evidence of one of the most beautiful moves in wrestling. Frankie Kazarian has been at the top of his game for years now. Like Daniels, he has never broken through as a world champion but Kazarian is a highlight of any show he is on. He shines with high risk moves but has the intelligence which comes from his years in the business to wrestle smart. The blend of Christopher Daniels and Kazarian is close to perfection.

The Claire Lynch secret brought Bad Influence together and showed the kinds of depths that these two occasionally vile men will go to. Initially they made up stories of infidelity between Styles and TNA President Dixie Carter, and then between Styles and Lynch, all of which turned out to be pure fabrication. But amongst all the drama, TNA had found itself a ridiculously entertaining tag team. Winning the TNA Tag Team Championships twice and defending them against the likes of Samoa Joe & Magnus, AJ Styles & Kurt Angle and Chavo Guerrero & Hernandez, Bad Influence have become a tight, well-oiled unit whose teamwork is as good as any in TNA history. As talented as they are, they are also not afraid to throw in a cheap shot when the ref's back is turned.

In 2013, Daniels and Kazarian have become involved in a war of words and of egos with Bobby Roode & Austin Aries. In fact, the only thing Roode & Aries agree on is that they don't like Bad Influence. Whilst the teams have collided and traded victories, fans watching the rivalry play out on TV are hyped for the prospect of the matches we could see. This feud has the potential to rival the hottest tag feuds in TNA history and could once again put the tag team scene in TNA back in the main event picture.

TNA
ONE NIGHT ONLY
02.08.13 10 REUNION

Arguably, this was the most stacked show yet of any of TNA's One Night Only offerings. Celebrating the last ten years, TNA highlighted some of the key feuds of its recent history.

With at least 4 PPV calibre main events on offer, fans in attendance were treated to several dream matches and rematches featuring no less than 8 TNA World Heavyweight Champions. For One Night Only, old feuds were rekindled and battle lines were drawn.

RESULTS

- Triple Threat Match Kenny King def. Petey Williams and Sonjay Dutt

- Velvet Sky def. Gail Kim

- Gauntlet Battle Royal – Matt Morgan outlasted Johnny Swinger, Johnny Devine, Shark Boy, Cassidy Riley, Robbie E, Jessie Godderz, Mr. Anderson and Joseph Park.

- Triple Threat Tag Team Match Aces & Eights Team 3D def. LAX (Homicide & Hernandez) and Bad Influence (Kazarian & Christopher Daniels)

- Jeff Hardy def. Austin Aries

- Bobby Roode def. James Storm

- Main Event - Kurt Angle def. Samoa Joe

JEREMY BORASH: James Storm has left his trademark cowboy hat in the maze. Can you help him navigate his way to retrieve it? Check on page 60 for the answer.

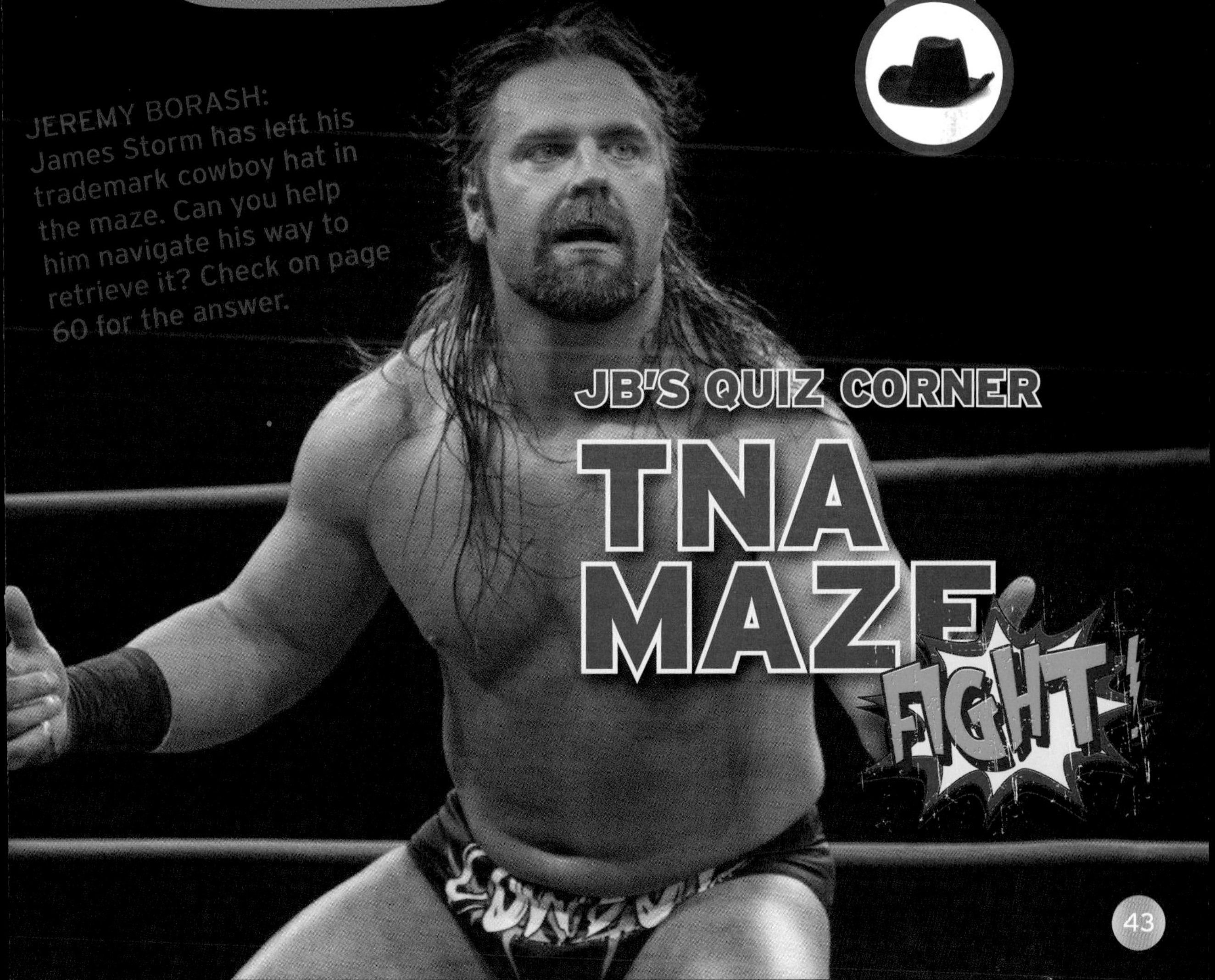

JB'S QUIZ CORNER

TNA MAZE

FIGHT!

43

Few could have imagined the effect of losing one triple threat match at Turning Point 2012 would have on the career and life of AJ Styles. It wasn't any ordinary match, however. Stipulated in the rules was that the loser of the fall would not be able to compete for the TNA World Heavyweight Championship for at least one calendar year. It would be a Turning Point in Styles' career.

PROFILE

AJ STYLES

(@AJSTYLESORG)

HEIGHT: 5'11"

WEIGHT: 215LBS

FROM: GAINESVILLE, GEORGIA

FINISHING MOVE: THE STYLES CLASH

As a TNA original and a former 4 time world Champion, this was one ruling that hurt...a lot. The next month, AJ lost again in what was billed as the final singles encounter with long time TNA rival, Christopher Daniels. Losing this match took Styles to a breaking point. Growing tired of being the good guy and doing things the honest way, AJ Styles told the world that he was sick of how things had gone and from now on he would be looking out for number one, and doing things his way. As a well known devout Christian, this reaction caught many off guard. With that proclamation, AJ Styles vanished from our TV screens.

Two months passed before TNA cameras attempted to track down 'The Phenomenal' one. During interviews conducted at his home, a friend and his wife Wendy told that AJ was a changed man. The pressures of losing any future title match for a year, losing to Daniels and the whole Clare Lynch saga where AJ had been accused of having an affair, had really taken its toll.

It became clear when we saw AJ Styles return to Impact Wrestling a month later, AJ had the look of a troubled man. Hair unkempt, unshaven and generally looking downbeat, fans wondered what had happened.

When he turned on James Storm during his return, having just seconds earlier saved Storm from an attack by Bad Influence, it was apparent that this was a man in conflict. Keeping silent he refused to offer any reason for his actions, only continuing to walk his own path, keeping people guessing as to his motives.

At times, it seemed he may have aligned himself with Aces & Eights, but that was also soon put to bed. The lack of comment means that no one truly knows what is going on in the mind of AJ Styles.

> "THE LACK OF COMMENT MEANS THAT NO ONE TRULY KNOWS WHAT IS GOING ON IN THE MIND OF AJ STYLES."

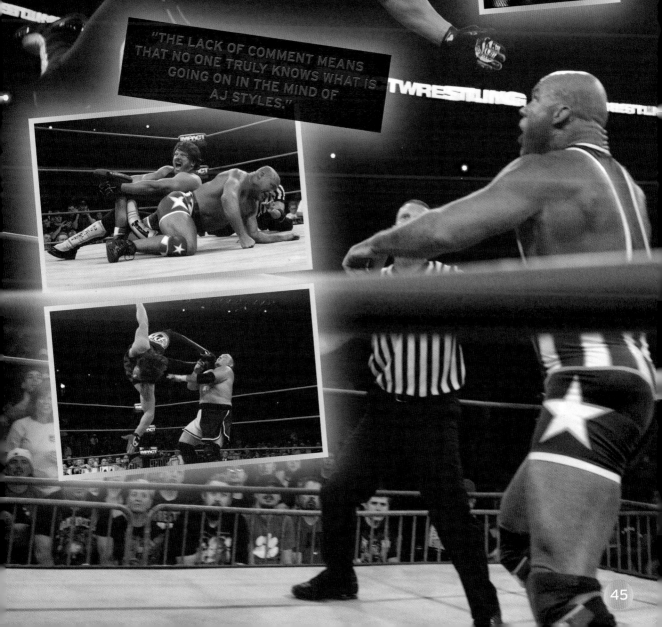

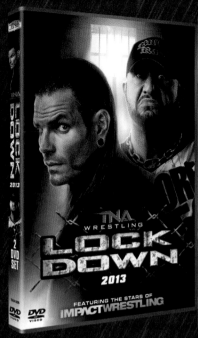
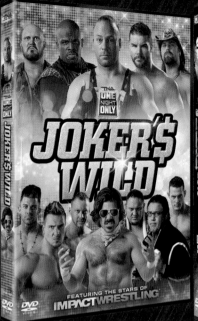
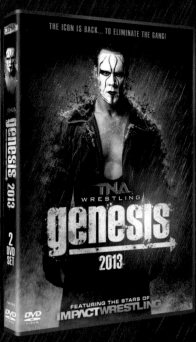

```
R  C  R  E  D  N  E  R  R  U  S  O  N  K  H  N
N  D  N  R  N  R  D  H  L  L  D  M  T  Y  A  D
O  F  R  J  G  K  T  Z  O  R  D  M  R  T  R  S
I  B  C  P  Z  Q  V  C  V  K  O  O  T  N  D  L
T  R  K  T  N  B  K  Z  L  Z  L  K  T  I  C  A
U  B  J  Q  W  D  M  G  K  G  L  D  F  O  O  M
L  E  X  G  O  C  M  P  R  W  A  X  L  P  R  M
O  D  C  W  E  M  L  O  V  O  T  N  D  G  E  I
S  X  N  I  R  N  F  R  R  R  S  K  M  N  J  V
E  X  B  L  F  D  E  Y  F  Q  N  X  K  I  U  E
R  X  T  W  N  I  R  S  N  L  I  B  V  N  S  R
L  B  X  U  R  O  R  T  I  B  A  T  K  R  T  S
A  K  O  L  T  T  C  M  S  G  J  P  U  I  A
N  B  N  C  M  F  Z  J  A  K  A  R  Q  T  C  R
I  L  I  F  K  P  H  P  M  S  R  P  B  N  E  Y
F  V  L  Q  D  E  S  T  I  N  A  T  I  O  N  X
```

AgainstAllOdds

BoundforGlory

DestinationX

FinalResolution

Genesis

HardcoreJustice

Lockdown

NoSurrender

Sacrifice

Slammiversary

Turning Point

VictoryRoad

WORDSEARCH 2

Find the words in the grid.
Words can go horizontally,
vertically and diagonally in
all eight directions.

Answers on page 60-61.

Arguably the greatest in-ring competitor still active in wrestling today, the Olympic hero, Kurt Angle, has been there and done it all in TNA. In recent times, he has taken some of the younger blood of the industry under his wing in an effort to impart some of his knowledge on them. His main protégé was Wes Brisco. With a common background in amateur wrestling it was the perfect match, but things were not as they appeared. Once Angle had got Brisco in the door as part of the Gut Check, Wes betrayed his mentor and was revealed as one of the masked member of the Aces & Eights group.

More recently, the confrontation between the Olympic gold medallist and former MMA champion Quinton 'Rampage' Jackson set tongues wagging. The potential of a feud between the two will set the world's eyes on Impact Wrestling, where Angle would be able to utilise that amateur background in the ring. It has benefitted Angle throughout his career and has always been the basis for his approach in the ring.

Kurt Angle has put his support behind amateur wrestling and in backing the campaign to reinstate it as one the sports of the Olympic Games, following its recent demotion. The role of amateur wrestling in professional wrestling is never more evident than in a Kurt Angle match. But Angle, in his 14 years in the business has brought every other aspect of his repertoire up to the same gold medal standard. A world class mat technician, and submission specialist, Kurt Angle is now a recognised TNA Hall of Famer and that is REAL.

"A WORLD CLASS MAT TECHNICIAN, AND SUBMISSION SPECIALIST."

HEIGHT: 6'0"

WEIGHT: 240LBS

FROM: PITTSBURGH, PENNSYLVANIA

FINISHING MOVE: THE ANGLE SLAM

PROFILE
KURT ANGLE

(@REALKURTANGLE)

He made it to the top of the mountain and then did what so many do, he became a jerk. For some men, holding the most prestigious title in the company creates a positive change but for Bobby Roode, it led to him becoming more ruthless, more aggressive, more obnoxious and more antagonistic than ever before. And boy was he good at it.

If he wasn't screwing over former Beer Money partner James Storm, he was lambasting anyone who got in his way, even TNA President Dixie Carter. Bobby Roode's historic run with the TNA World Heavyweight championship was finally ended in 2012, by the man who would become his tag team partner in 2013. With Austin Aries, Roode may have found his best tag team partner ever. Already the team comprising of the two biggest egos in professional wrestling have captured the TNA Tag Team titles, but it's the potential of a long running series with Bad Influence that has many fans hoping Roode and Aries can survive together long enough to see that happen.

Perhaps the break from the world title picture will benefit Roode as since dropping the strap, his latest attempts have all come up short. Refocusing his efforts on the foundations of what elevated the 'Leader of the Selfish Generation' to stardom, the tag team ranks, should mean not only more tag team gold but also more singles gold in Bobby Roode's future. At the very least you can be 100% sure that the inevitable implosion of his partnership with Aries will relight their epic feud.

> "YOU CAN BE 100% SURE THAT THE INEVITABLE IMPLOSION OF HIS PARTNERSHIP WITH ARIES WILL RELIGHT THEIR EPIC FEUD."

HEIGHT: 6'0"

WEIGHT: 240LBS

FROM: TORONTO, CANADA

FINISHING MOVE: THE PAY OFF

PROFILE
BOBBY ROODE

 (@REALBOBBYROODE)

The 'Man' of the X Division scene, Kenny King has taken it upon himself to freshen things up. The party man from Las Vegas loves to have a good time and wants everyone else to have one too. The confidence oozes from King before every match and he carries himself as a star. But it's not been an easy road for Kenny King. Already in his short time in TNA he has had to battle back from high profile defeats against Christian York and in several matches with then X Division champion Rob Van Dam. In one last attempt, where should he fail, King would have been thrown out of the X Division; Kenny King rose to the challenge and finally defeated the Hardcore Legend RVD.

As the top dog of the division whilst as champion, Kenny King became a target for everyone else. Losing the title to Chris Sabin at Slammiversary might thus prove to be a blessing. The making of the man is not how many times he loses, but is in how many times he gets back up. It's now up to Kenny King to show how good he can be. We believe this rising star will continue to shine and this is just the start of great things to come. Long live the King.

> "KENNY KING ROSE TO THE CHALLENGE AND FINALLY DEFEATED THE HARDCORE LEGEND RVD."

HEIGHT: 6'0"

WEIGHT: 230lbs

FROM: Las Vegas, Nevada

FINISHING MOVE: The Royal Flush

PROFILE
KENNY KING

 (@KENNYKINGPINANX)

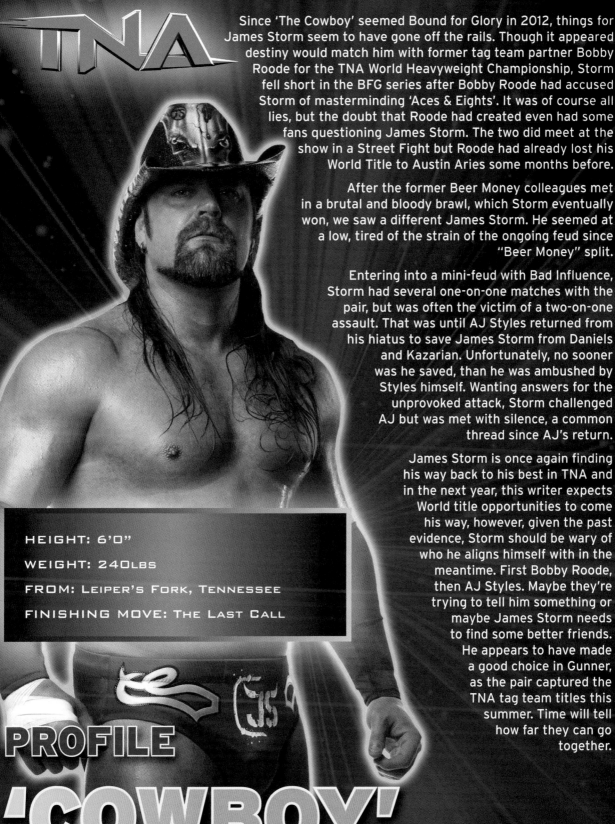

Since 'The Cowboy' seemed Bound for Glory in 2012, things for James Storm seem to have gone off the rails. Though it appeared destiny would match him with former tag team partner Bobby Roode for the TNA World Heavyweight Championship, Storm fell short in the BFG series after Bobby Roode had accused Storm of masterminding 'Aces & Eights'. It was of course all lies, but the doubt that Roode had created even had some fans questioning James Storm. The two did meet at the show in a Street Fight but Roode had already lost his World Title to Austin Aries some months before.

After the former Beer Money colleagues met in a brutal and bloody brawl, which Storm eventually won, we saw a different James Storm. He seemed at a low, tired of the strain of the ongoing feud since "Beer Money" split.

Entering into a mini-feud with Bad Influence, Storm had several one-on-one matches with the pair, but was often the victim of a two-on-one assault. That was until AJ Styles returned from his hiatus to save James Storm from Daniels and Kazarian. Unfortunately, no sooner was he saved, than he was ambushed by Styles himself. Wanting answers for the unprovoked attack, Storm challenged AJ but was met with silence, a common thread since AJ's return.

James Storm is once again finding his way back to his best in TNA and in the next year, this writer expects World title opportunities to come his way, however, given the past evidence, Storm should be wary of who he aligns himself with in the meantime. First Bobby Roode, then AJ Styles. Maybe they're trying to tell him something or maybe James Storm needs to find some better friends. He appears to have made a good choice in Gunner, as the pair captured the TNA tag team titles this summer. Time will tell how far they can go together.

HEIGHT: 6'0"

WEIGHT: 240lbs

FROM: Leiper's Fork, Tennessee

FINISHING MOVE: The Last Call

PROFILE

'COWBOY' JAMES STORM

(@COWBOY_J_STORM)

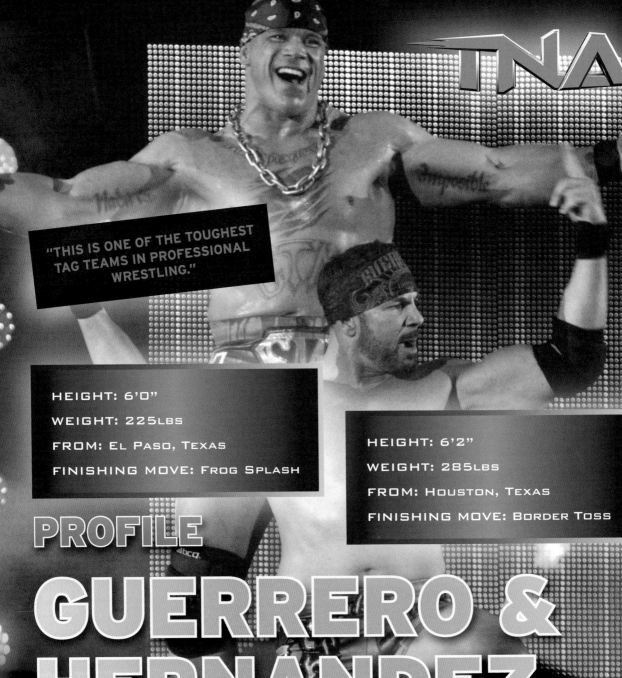

"THIS IS ONE OF THE TOUGHEST TAG TEAMS IN PROFESSIONAL WRESTLING."

HEIGHT: 6'0"

WEIGHT: 225LBS

FROM: EL PASO, TEXAS

FINISHING MOVE: Frog Splash

HEIGHT: 6'2"

WEIGHT: 285LBS

FROM: HOUSTON, TEXAS

FINISHING MOVE: Border Toss

PROFILE

GUERRERO & HERNANDEZ

(@MEXWARRIOR) (@TNASUPERMEX)

The 'Mexican Warrior' and 'Super Mex' became aligned shortly after the Mexican Legend Chavo Guerrero signed with TNA. It was a natural fit. Both were American-born Mexicans, one was small in stature but had the speed, technical prowess and high-flying abilities in the ring, and the other had agility, size and unbelievable power. Together this tag team covered all bases. And in the ring they proved it. Defeating the super-talented team of Bad Influence to lift their first TNA Tag Team Championship, was an impressive feat, especially as they had only been teaming for a few months. That they also overcame Kurt Angle and

AJ Styles in the same match was all the more impressive. As the months progressed, the pairing of Guerrero and Hernandez honed their skills as a team and continued to beat any team that TNA threw their way. On the Manchester show of Impact Wrestling they finally lost the straps to the impromptu team of Bobby Roode and Austin Aries, though they would eventually regain them months later, again in another triple threat match. Whether they are holding the gold or chasing it, this is one of the toughest tag teams in professional wrestling and will never be far off another title run.

Predicted by many to be the first British-born TNA World Heavyweight Champion, Magnus has a lot to live up to. But if he is to get himself into the title picture, he must first combat the evil Aces & Eights. The renegade group have been a thorn in Magnus' side for most of 2013. Having previously assaulted Magnus with the ball-pen hammer in 2012, it seems the group were not done with the former UK Gladiator. Back for more, Magnus found himself some allies in the form of Sting, Eric Young, James Storm and his former tag team champion partner Samoa Joe inside Lethal Lockdown, where Team TNA emerged victorious. The rekindled partnership with Samoa Joe may be something to look out for in the coming months. However, with both men being entered into the Bound for Glory series, a rivalry between the two would be equally as exciting. Magnus will be considered an outsider for the Bound for Glory Series based purely on the other wrestlers involved, but Magnus is close to becoming a break out star in TNA. This could be his year.

" MAGNUS IS CLOSE TO BECOMING A BREAK OUT STAR IN TNA. THIS COULD BE HIS YEAR."

HEIGHT: 6'3"

WEIGHT: 240lbs

FROM: King's Lynn, UK

FINISHING MOVE: The Tormentum

PROFILE
MAGNUS

(@MAGNUSOFFICIAL)

'The Icon' of professional wrestling is the cornerstone of TNA Impact Wrestling. With nearly 30 years in the business, there is nothing that Sting hasn't seen or done. A multiple time World Champion including the TNA World Heavyweight Championship on 4 different occasions, in 2012, Sting also became the first inductee into the TNA Hall of Fame. As the first inductee it was an amazing honour for Sting, but for the fans it was a chance to say thank you for the years of service to TNA. There is no doubt that Sting's association with the promotion gave TNA a lot of credibility early on. But Sting is by no means done in the ring. At Slammiversary, he returned to face World Champion Bully Ray in the main event. Seeking retribution for the attack by Ray's group Aces & Eights months earlier, Sting came so close to snatching the gold that but for Bully Ray's underhand tactics, we might have had a new champion. Ultimately in defeat, as per the stipulation of the match, Sting will not be able to wrestle for the TNA title again. Where that leaves Sting is up in the air. As a legend and locker room leader, Sting is the ideal man to pass on his years of knowledge of the mat game to the young up and coming stars of tomorrow.

HEIGHT: 6'2"

WEIGHT: 250lbs

FROM: VENICE BEACH, CALIFORNIA

FINISHING MOVE: SCORPION DEATH LOCK

PROFILE

'THE ICON' STING

 (@STING)

"THERE IS NOTHING THAT STING HASN'T SEEN OR DONE."

There is a big difference between BEING the show and RUNNING the show. Since Hulk Hogan's in-ring career has wound down we have seen the Hulkster take a prominent role in the TNA office. Acting as TNA President Dixie Carter's advisor, Hogan has become the boss for a lot of aspects of Impact Wrestling. Finding the balance between keeping the fans happy and doing what is right for the business has proved to be a much tougher task than Hulk could ever imagine. No stranger to the lies and deceit of fellow wrestlers even the biggest star in wrestling history did not see coming, the trail of untruths told by his son-in-law Bully Ray. Playing Hogan as a pawn in his game to become TNA World Champion, Bully Ray really overstepped the line by playing with the heart of Hulk's daughter Brooke. Though he's not as young as he once was, we believe we may not have seen the last of hulkamania running wild in TNA. Bully Ray may want to be careful what he wishes for.

> "BULLY RAY REALLY OVERSTEPPED THE LINE BY PLAYING WITH THE HEART OF HULK'S DAUGHTER BROOKE."

PROFILE

'THE IMMORTAL' HULK HOGAN

HEIGHT: 6'7"

WEIGHT: 302lbs

FROM: Venice Beach, California

FINISHING MOVE: Atomic Leg Drop

🐦 (@HULKHOGAN)

TNA

IMPACT WRESTLING

Sundays 9pm

CHALLENGE

Sky: Ch 145, Freeview: Ch 46, Virgin: Ch 139

57

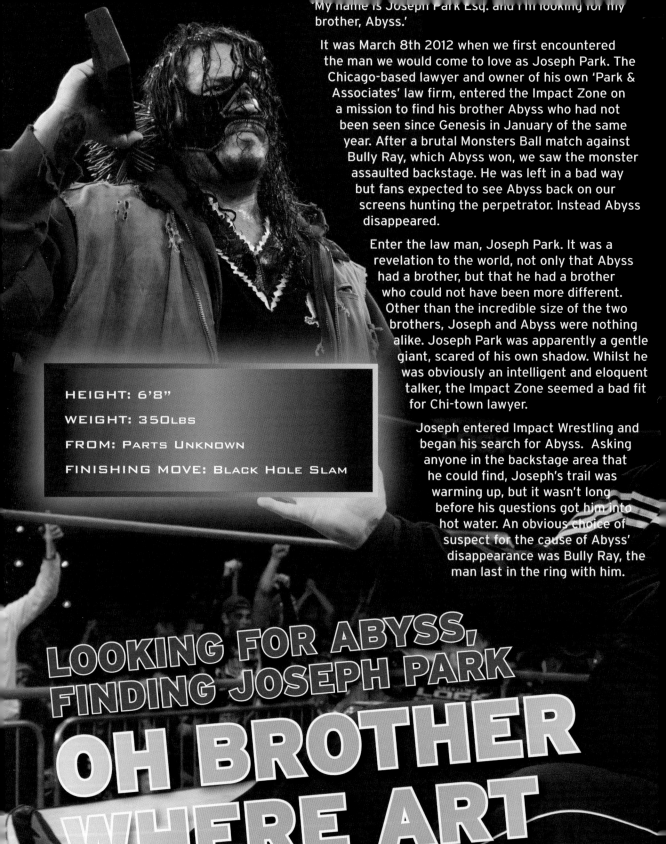

'My name is Joseph Park Esq. and I'm looking for my brother, Abyss.'

It was March 8th 2012 when we first encountered the man we would come to love as Joseph Park. The Chicago-based lawyer and owner of his own 'Park & Associates' law firm, entered the Impact Zone on a mission to find his brother Abyss who had not been seen since Genesis in January of the same year. After a brutal Monsters Ball match against Bully Ray, which Abyss won, we saw the monster assaulted backstage. He was left in a bad way but fans expected to see Abyss back on our screens hunting the perpetrator. Instead Abyss disappeared.

Enter the law man, Joseph Park. It was a revelation to the world, not only that Abyss had a brother, but that he had a brother who could not have been more different. Other than the incredible size of the two brothers, Joseph and Abyss were nothing alike. Joseph Park was apparently a gentle giant, scared of his own shadow. Whilst he was obviously an intelligent and eloquent talker, the Impact Zone seemed a bad fit for Chi-town lawyer.

Joseph entered Impact Wrestling and began his search for Abyss. Asking anyone in the backstage area that he could find, Joseph's trail was warming up, but it wasn't long before his questions got him into hot water. An obvious choice of suspect for the cause of Abyss' disappearance was Bully Ray, the man last in the ring with him.

HEIGHT: 6'8"

WEIGHT: 350LBS

FROM: PARTS UNKNOWN

FINISHING MOVE: BLACK HOLE SLAM

LOOKING FOR ABYSS, FINDING JOSEPH PARK

OH BROTHER WHERE ART THOU?

Bully Ray vehemently denied he played any part in Abyss going missing and challenged Park to a match. What was Joseph letting himself in for?

Having never set foot into a ring in his life, that was his brother's domain, Joseph Park looked a fish out of water in an 'Anything Goes Match'. What he lacked in ability, he made up for with heart and withstood the onslaught of Bully Ray. In a surprising turn of events during the match, whilst Park hid under the ring, Abyss made a brief return to Choke Slam Ray through a table, allowing his brother to pick up a shock victory.

Abyss once more vanished and so Joseph's search went on leading him deeper into the heart of wrestling.

Falling in love with the sport, Park asked to be allowed to train to be a wrestler down in TNA's developmental promotion Ohio Valley Wrestling. During Open Fight Night it was Park who came back to Impact Wrestling to face Robbie E. Park was victorious once more but this was on his own. It meant so much to him.

But just as Joseph Park was beginning to make a name for himself, the monster Abyss made another shocking return to Impact Wrestling on May 9th 2013 as the surprise third member of a team with Sting and Kurt Angle vs. Aces & Eights. Decimating Devon and Bully Ray before putting Mr. Anderson through a table, Aces & Eights seem that they might have actually met their match and someone who can finally even the odds for TNA, something further underlined at Slammiversary where Abyss beat Devon for the TNA TV title.

But so many questions are still unanswered. Where has Abyss been? Is he here to stay? And what does this mean for the Aces & Eights? With so much still to discover, TNA will be an intriguing place to be. What is certain though, out of all the controversy surrounding the disappearance of Abyss, the TNA faithful have been won over by the charming, bumbling brother. Whilst we don't know about the future of Abyss, I think Joseph Park is here to stay.

"WHERE HAS ABYSS BEEN? IS HE HERE TO STAY? AND WHAT DOES THIS MEAN FOR THE ACES & EIGHTS?"

HEIGHT: 6'8"

WEIGHT: 350LBS

FROM: CHICAGO, ILLINOIS

FINISHING MOVE: THE CROSS-EXAMINER

P6 & 7 THE CHAMP IS HERE!

1. KURT ANGLE

2. BOBBY ROODE

3. AUSTIN ARIES

4. MR.ANDERSON

5. BULLY RAY

6. STING

7. JAMES STORM

8. AJ STYLES

P22 TNA CROSSWORD

```
                              J E R E M Y B O R A S H
                              R               C
              M               E               E
      D I S Q U A L I F I C A T I O N         S
          M   Y           G       M   B A D I N F L U E N C E
      A   H   H       S   A                   N   A
      S L A M M I V E R S A R Y               D   N
      S   Y   H       Y   L   I       R       E   D
      O   H   E       L   K       C H A L L E N G E
      C   E   M       U   I       C   O       I
      I   M   M   E U R O S T O R E         G H T
      A       M   M   M   J   K   S   T       S
      T F     E   M   B O B B Y R O O D E
      E I   G L A S G O W   K   A   R
        G   L           J O K E R   S
        H   A               E       P
        T   S G L A S G O W         U D
                                    B U L L Y R A Y
              M A G N U S           D
```

ANSWERS

P18 SPOT THE DIFFERENCE

P35 JB'S TNA QUIZ CORNER

1. BOBBY ROODE

2. DEVON

3. STING AND KURT ANGLE

4. KNOCKOUT KNOCKDOWN

5. KING'S LYNN

6. WEMBLEY

7. SUNDAY, CHALLENGE TV

8. THE BLOSSOM TWINS

9. TOMMY DREAMER

10. MOTOR CITY MACHINE GUNS

11. KAZARIAN

12. MIKE TENAY

13. GENESIS, LOCKDOWN, SLAMMIVERSARY, BOUND FOR GLORY

14. JAY BRADLEY

15. TARYN TERRELL

P43 TNA MAZE

START

P29 WORDSEARCH 1

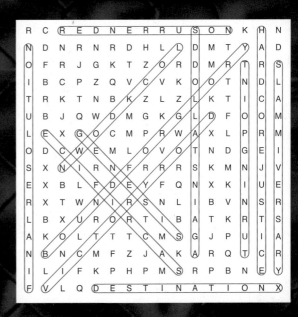

P47 WORDSEARCH 2

WHERE'S BOBBY ROODE?